W9-BEP-467

EXTREME CAREERS™

TREASURE HUNTERS

Corona Brezina

rosen publishing's
rosen
central®

New York

Published in 2009 by The Rosen Publishing Group, Inc.
29 East 21st Street, New York, NY 10010

Library of Congress Cataloging-in-Publication Data

Brezina, Corona.
Treasure hunters / Corona Brezina. — 1st ed.
    p. cm.—(Extreme careers)
Includes bibliographical references and index.
ISBN-13: 978-1-4042-1788-1 (library binding)
1. Treasure troves. 2. Treasure troves—Vocational guidance. I. Title.
G525.B8126 2009
622'.19—dc22

                                                    2008010298

Manufactured in Malaysia

On the cover: Emerald treasure hunter James King Hill holds a handful of emeralds he found in a mine.

Contents

Introduction

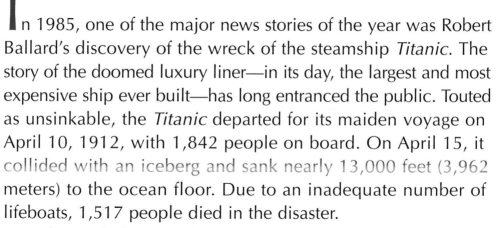

In 1985, one of the major news stories of the year was Robert Ballard's discovery of the wreck of the steamship *Titanic*. The story of the doomed luxury liner—in its day, the largest and most expensive ship ever built—has long entranced the public. Touted as unsinkable, the *Titanic* departed for its maiden voyage on April 10, 1912, with 1,842 people on board. On April 15, it collided with an iceberg and sank nearly 13,000 feet (3,962 meters) to the ocean floor. Due to an inadequate number of lifeboats, 1,517 people died in the disaster.

Video and photographs taken by Ballard's team revealed an otherworldly scene. The mangled remains of the once opulent ship were surrounded by a debris field of wreckage that was scattered with personal belongings of the passengers. A tiny remotely operated vehicle (ROV) swam inside the ship and took photos of the interior. The team also retrieved artifacts using their submersible's manipulator arms.

Ballard held the opinion that the wreck was a grave site and should remain undisturbed, but exploration—and public

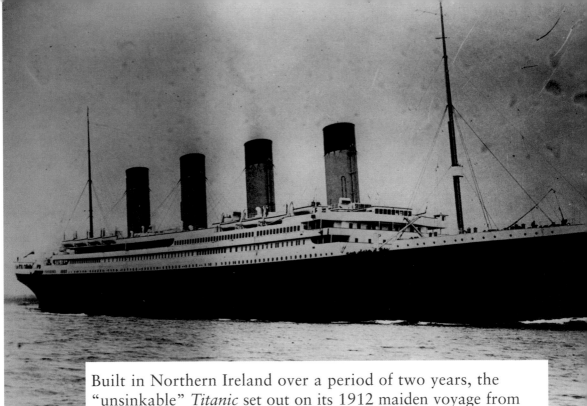

Built in Northern Ireland over a period of two years, the "unsinkable" *Titanic* set out on its 1912 maiden voyage from Southampton, England, bound for New York City.

fascination—of the *Titanic* has continued. More artifacts have been recovered, ranging from documents and pieces of jewelry to a huge section of the hull. People flock to exhibits of *Titanic* relics.

Professional treasure hunters share this fascination with lost ships. They're in it for the money, of course, but they are also motivated by the thrill of discovery. Shipwrecks are sometimes described as "time capsules" since newly discovered wrecks have been untouched by humans since the time they sank. Collectors are willing to pay extra for that historical connection. A gold piece from the sunken Spanish galleon *Atocha*, for example, is worth far more than the value of its weight.

Robert Ballard used a remotely operated vehicle (ROV) to capture pictures of the *Titanic*'s interior. It was fitted with powerful lights to cut through the near-total darkness.

A treasure hunter has to be willing to take risks. A treasure hunter must also be versatile, since he or she will have to feel at home at the helm of a boat, at the site of a wreck, in a library poring over old historical texts, and in front of a group of potential investors. Tracking down a wreck takes detective skills and tenacity. A bad day can involve hurricanes, accidents, equipment malfunctions, and unscrupulous rivals. Still, the lure of treasure wins out in the end. Treasure hunting is one of the rare jobs where a successful day at work may literally be rewarded with bars of gold.

Spanish Treasure and Sunken Pirate Hoards

For almost three hundred years—from about 1500 to 1800—Spanish ships called galleons carried cargoes of gold, silver, and other valuables from Mexico and South America to Europe. Spain was one of the great world powers during this era. Hundreds of galleons, however, were shipwrecked and lost, many within sight of land. To this day, relatively few of these have been located and salvaged.

On a few occasions, entire treasure fleets met disaster at sea. The most famous was the 1715 Spanish treasure fleet, a group of twelve ships traveling from Cuba to Spain. About a week after they set sail, a hurricane hit. Eleven of the ships were dashed to pieces off the coast of Florida and lost. About 1,200 people died. Spain sent teams to salvage the wrecks, but their equipment was not sufficient to retrieve treasure from the seafloor. In addition, they had to contend with looters and pirates who plundered the site for years. Eventually, though, the wreck and the treasure were mostly forgotten.

In 1948, a building contractor named Kip Wagner was astonished to realize that blackened nuggets he found on a beach near his Florida home were actually silver coins. Over the years, Wagner pursued the history behind his discovery and became one of the pioneering modern treasure hunters. He obtained a permit to explore the 1715 wrecks and organized a team of divers to check out the underwater sites. By the time they had salvaged $1 million worth of silver coins, Wagner decided that it was time to formally establish a company for his salvage work. He called it the Real Eight Company. When he died in 1972, Wagner was the first person to have become a millionaire through hunting down treasure ships.

Nuestra Señora de Atocha

In September 1622, a treasure fleet of twenty-eight galleons sailed for Spain from the New World. Before they had been at sea for two days, a hurricane struck and sank eight of the ships near the Florida Keys. Five hundred and fifty people died. Among the wrecked ships were the *Nuestra Señora de Atocha* and the *Santa Margarita*, both carrying a fortune of gold, silver, and gems. Desperate, the Spanish attempted to salvage the cargo. In early October, however, another hurricane swept away all traces of the lost treasure ships.

The *Atocha* and *Margarita* remained hidden—and shrouded in legend—for centuries. Then, in 1966, a treasure hunter named Mel Fisher embarked on a quest to find the two long-lost galleons.

Three-masted ships known as galleons once transported bountiful cargoes of gold and silver to Spain, with a good number succumbing to violent weather, pirate attacks, or other perils of the ocean.

Mel Fisher had been fascinated with treasure and diving from his youth. In the 1950s, he opened one of the nation's first scuba shops out of a feed shed on a chicken farm in California. He gave scuba diving lessons and shot underwater films as a sideline, and in 1960, he mounted his first treasure expedition. Fisher gradually built up a skilled treasure hunting team. In 1963, they relocated to Florida, which offered far richer opportunities for treasure hunters. For a time, Fisher was one of Kip Wagner's business partners.

Fisher made headway in his search for the *Atocha* in 1970, when he began collaborating with Eugene Lyon, a maritime historian. Lyon tracked down records from the seventeenth century in Spanish archives that described the recovery effort immediately after the loss of the galleons. He realized that one island near the site of the wreck had been renamed shortly after the disaster, information that helped narrow down the area of the search.

In 1973, a diver from Fisher's team found three gold bars that were identified as belonging to the *Atocha*'s cargo. Fisher was on the right track. Over the next few years, divers also recovered part of the hull of the *Atocha*'s sister ship, the *Margarita*, as well as gold and artifacts worth millions. But the *Atocha* remained elusive.

A breakthrough appeared to be imminent in July 1975, when Mel Fisher's son Dirk discovered nine brass cannons belonging to the *Atocha*. The team celebrated, believing that the bulk of the treasure would be nearby. A few days later, however, tragedy struck. One of the search boats capsized unexpectedly. Three people were trapped in their cabins and died in the accident—Dirk Fisher; his wife, Angel; and a diver named Rick Gage.

Mel Fisher was devastated, but he kept up his resolve. He believed that his son would not have wanted him to abandon the search. Fisher would often begin work with the cry, "Today's the day!" His enthusiasm and determination kept his team optimistic, even during the times that Fisher ran out of money and could not pay them. The search stretched on for years.

Pieces of the *Atocha*'s cargo had been scattered across a large area of the ocean floor. In May 1985, a diver found a ballast

Mel Fisher—scuba diving pioneer, charismatic entrepreneur, and treasure hunting legend—displays some of the riches recovered from the wreck of the *Atocha*.

stone that had been stowed in the *Atocha*'s hold to provide stability and balance. Nearby, the team uncovered gold bars and chains, silver, sixteen emeralds, and other artifacts. They believed that the main treasure might be nearby, but it was a false hope. The next day, they made no further discoveries.

Spanish treasure ships often carried gold and silver bars and coins called pieces of eight. Their name came from the fact that they were worth eight reals, a monetary unit.

On July 20, 1985, a diver on a routine search noticed an unusual mound nearby. Upon examination, he realized that it was a huge pile of silver bars. Mel Fisher's son Kane radioed his father, telling him to put away the charts because the treasure had been found. The sixteen-year search had finally paid off.

Over the next year, divers brought up millions of dollars worth of gold, silver, and emeralds, as well as artifacts such as tools, pottery, personal items, and timbers of the ship's hull. Based on historical records, Fisher had estimated that the *Atocha*'s treasure could be worth $400 million. The recovery of the *Atocha*'s treasure is an ongoing project that will continue for years.

The Pirate Ship *Whydah*

In addition to hurricanes, the Spanish galleons and other treasure ships had to contend with pirates. They were the terrorists of their age; contemporary books and movies that romanticize pirates do not convey how much citizens dreaded their cruelty and destructiveness. One pirate legend, however, has been proven true in a few instances: there really is sunken pirate treasure waiting to be found by intrepid treasure hunters. One of the most famous instances was the salvage of the pirate Samuel Bellamy's ship, the *Whydah*.

Samuel Bellamy—known as Black Sam after the color of his wild hair—was one of the most notorious pirate captains of his day. In February 1717, his crew seized the *Whydah*, a British slave ship. The galley had just sold its human cargo in Jamaica, and when Bellamy captured it, it was carrying ivory, sugar, and gold.

Over the next few months, the *Whydah's* crew plundered about half a dozen more ships, amassing a fortune in gold and silver. But on April 26, Bellamy's luck ran out. A gale hit the *Whydah* as it sailed off the coast of Cape Cod, Massachusetts, and the ship crashed into a sandbar. According to historical records, over the next few weeks, residents from the surrounding area swarmed the beaches to scavenge treasure from wreckage that washed ashore.

"Black Sam" Bellamy was himself a treasure hunter. After the 1715 Spanish treasure fleet foundered, he was among the opportunists who hoped to make their fortune salvaging the wreckage.

Centuries later, Barry Clifford began to doubt that the *Whydah*'s story was truly finished. He reasoned that in the early spring, when the *Whydah* sunk, the water would have been too frigid for diving or even wading out to the wreckage. He thought that the remains of the *Whydah*—and the bulk of her treasure—were still buried off the shore.

Growing up in Cape Cod, young Barry Clifford had heard tales of Black Sam's shipwreck. Clifford had a passion for adventure and the outdoors. After majoring in history and sociology in college, he returned to Massachusetts. It seemed natural to return to his pursuit of the *Whydah*.

Clifford had considerable diving experience, but when he mounted his search in earnest, he started out by combing through history books and archives of documents. His most tantalizing find was the papers of Captain Cyprian Southack, the mapmaker assigned by the governor of the province of Massachusetts Bay to investigate and salvage the *Whydah*. Southack had scouted out the scene of the wreck, interviewed residents, and drawn maps of the area. Clifford retraced Southack's steps and tried to pinpoint the present-day location of some of Southack's landmarks that had vanished.

By 1983, Clifford was ready for the hunt. He had gotten his permits, bought a dive boat called the *Vast Explorer*, and lined up investors. He consulted with Mel Fisher, who was still engaged in his search for the *Atocha*. The former president's son John F. Kennedy Jr. even signed up for a stint as a mate on the *Vast Explorer*. Clifford's crew started scanning the seafloor with a

Underwater Hazards

Wreck diving is not for the faint of heart. Danger can present itself in various forms—drowning, sharks, poor visibility, hypothermia, equipment failure—and divers must be prepared for any contingency. Divers may have to battle strong currents or choppy water. They can get lost in dust raised during underwater exploration. They may become pinned down by pieces of wreckage. Many receive injuries or experience health problems as a result of diving. During his search for the *Whydah*, Barry Clifford went partially deaf in one ear as a result of so much diving.

Deep sea divers run further risks. At depths below about sixty-five feet (twenty meters), divers begin to experience what is known as nitrogen narcosis. Because of the high water pressure at that depth, the human body absorbs more nitrogen than on land. A diver experiencing nitrogen narcosis has difficulty with thinking and coordination.

After spending time underwater in the deep sea, a diver must ascend slowly in order to allow the extra nitrogen to cycle out of the body. Usually, the diver slowly works his or her way up an anchor rope, pausing for periods at predetermined "decompression stops." If the diver ascends too quickly, large bubbles of nitrogen can form just outside of the bloodstream. This condition, decompression sickness or "the bends," is agonizingly painful and can have serious—even fatal—health consequences.

Barry Clifford brandishes a cannon ball found in 1998 among the wreckage of a fleet of pirate and French warships that sank off of Venezuela's coast about three centuries ago.

magnetometer, a device that detects the presence of iron. By the end of the summer, they had found no evidence of the *Whydah*, however, and some of the team members were growing discouraged. Clifford spent the winter planning new strategies and worrying about money.

The next spring, Clifford relaunched the search with newer, more sensitive equipment. On July 19, as a storm rolled in, a diver found three heavily encrusted cannons. In addition, Clifford found a Spanish coin—a valuable one-ounce silver coin known as a "piece of eight." Coincidentally, a news crew was filming the search that day.

Over the next few days, the divers found piles of silver coins and gold dust. They brought up treasure, artifacts, and even the leg bone of a pirate, but they still had no definitive proof that their find was indeed the *Whydah*. In October 1985, the crew raised a ship's bell encrusted in a large mass of debris (known as a concretion). After it was cleaned, the inscription "The *Whydah* Gally 1716" was revealed.

The treasure, worth over $5 million, included gold, silver, and jewelry, as well as firearms, swords, tools, navigational instruments, personal possessions, and components of the ship. In addition to the monetary worth, the discovery of the *Whydah* yielded valuable information about the everyday lives of pirates.

Clifford has gone on to discover other pirate ships, including the *Fiery Dragon* captained by Billy One-Hand, which went down in 1721. He still believes that the bulk of the *Whydah*'s treasure is somewhere under the ocean and continues to return to the site.

Other Treasures Beneath the Sea

The oceans and seas of the world are littered with shipwrecks. When salvagers are searching for a particular ship, they often find wrecks of others ships that had sunk in the area.

The oldest known shipwreck, dating from 2250 BCE, was found off the coast of one of the islands of Greece. Not surprisingly, the first record of treasure hunters diving down to wrecks occurs in the writings of a Greek historian, Herodotus, who lived during the fifth century BCE. Since then, the human fascination with sunken treasure has not diminished. Intrepid treasure hunters have identified ships from the ancient world all the way up to twentieth-century ocean liners and World War II submarines. They have explored wrecks that were buried for centuries and wrecks that sank miles down to the ocean floor. In some cases, a treasure hunting expedition turns into the adventure of a lifetime and yields a fortune. Some particularly hazardous regions are notorious as ship graveyards. North Carolina's Outer Banks, for example are littered with remnants of nearly seven hundred ships.

Raising the *Vasa*

For most treasure hunters, their quest is to retrieve a ship's valuable cargo. In the case of the Swedish *Vasa*, however, the ship itself was the treasure. In his book *Treasure Lost at Sea: Diving to the World's Great Shipwrecks*, the renowned marine archaeologist Robert F. Marx describes the raising of the *Vasa* as "the most ambitious underwater archaeological recovery ever made."

The *Vasa* was intended to be the flagship of Sweden's fleet of warships. Built in the 1620s, it was the world's largest ship and one of the most magnificent. It was richly decorated by carvings and paintings of characters from the Bible and mythology; its figurehead (a sculpture or carving affixed to the front of a ship) was a gilded lion. In 1628, the *Vasa* cast off in Stockholm Harbor on its maiden voyage and sailed majestically past cheering crowds. Before the *Vasa* even reached the open sea, though, a gust of wind caused it to lurch. It capsized and sank to the bottom of the harbor.

In 1953, Anders Franzén, a Swedish engineer, obtained permission to search for the *Vasa*. Over three summers of diving, he found nothing. People began to think he was a madman. Finally, in August 1956, he located the *Vasa*. Because of the cold temperatures and low salt content of the water, the wood of the ship had not disintegrated.

The warship *Vasa* is now open as a museum. During the recovery, divers found over ten thousand artifacts lying exactly where they had settled when the ship sank in 1628.

With the support of the Swedish navy and the Neptune Salvage Company, Franzén and the newly formed Vasa Committee planned the raising of the ship. They rejected ideas such as filling the *Vasa* with buoyant Ping-Pong balls, instead opting to raise it with a network of steel cables attached to pontoon boats. Once it neared the surface, divers sealed all of the holes and cracks in the ship, a project that lasted a year. Then the water was pumped out, and the *Vasa* rose to the surface. It was towed to a dry dock on a huge custom-built raft, and archaeologists and historians began the unprecedented task of preservation and restoration.

Today, the ship is displayed in a museum and is one of the national treasures of Sweden. People from across the world stop in to marvel at the historic warship. And conservators are kept busy with the ongoing task of preserving the *Vasa*.

California Gold on the *Central America*

In 1849, treasure hunters swarmed to California to make their fortune after gold was discovered near Sacramento. Many of these "forty-niners" later decided to return to the East Coast with their newfound riches. Since land travel was difficult and dangerous, they often booked passage on steamships.

One of these ships was the luxurious *Central America*, commanded by Captain William Lewis Herndon of the U.S. Navy. On September 8, the ship departed Havana, Cuba, for the last leg of the voyage to New York, carrying 578 people and over three tons of gold. In today's value, the gold was worth about $1 billion. The next day, amid hurricane winds, the ship began taking on water. By September 11, the ship was flooded, and the water had extinguished the steam engine. Captain Herndon ordered the crew to construct makeshift rafts from the ship's wooden interior. They began shuttling passengers to a nearby brig, the *Marine*, which had come to aid the *Central America*. But before the evacuation was completed, the steamship slipped beneath the roiling waves. The wreck claimed the lives of 425 people, including Captain Herndon. The loss of the gold contributed to an economic depression.

In the early 1980s, an oceanographic engineer named Tommy Thompson began to research the *Central America*. He pored over old records and newspaper accounts, and analyzed the data with a computer to narrow down the search site. Since the wreck had sunk deep down to the ocean floor—about 8,000 feet (2,438 meters), as it turned out—Thompson's team would have to use cutting-edge methods of exploration and retrieval. (Humans cannot dive that deep.) Along with his partners, Thompson began

Tens of thousands of people flocked to California during the gold rush. Between 1849 and 1868, the gold-fields may have yielded as much as $15 billion at today's prices.

designing a revolutionary remotely operated vehicle (ROV) that would work at the site of the wreck.

Thompson had spent a year working as a diver for Mel Fisher. He had learned a lot during this time, but he was critical of some of Fisher's practices. Thompson planned a methodical operation that took advantage of the latest technological advances.

A recently improved form of sonar made it possible for the team to scan the likely area over a period of forty days in 1986. Based on the images they obtained, they identified several possible locations. In September 1988, they made a positive identification of the *Central America*. Photos from their ROV's camera revealed piles of gold coins and bars.

The next year, they returned with a salvage ship. When weather permitted, they would run their ROV, named *Nemo*, around the clock. Since the contents of the ship were so valuable, the team could not risk damaging pieces during retrieval. The ROV had a nozzle that could coat a pile of gold or artifacts in a protective casing of silicone before grabbing it. In addition to coins, nuggets, and bars, *Nemo* brought up suitcases and other possessions of the passengers. Thompson also gave scientists a chance to use his equipment to study the marine life and geology of the site.

In total, Thompson's team retrieved over three tons of gold. Some of the coins retrieved were very rare, such as hundreds of $20 "double eagles." A single ingot was later sold at auction for $8 million.

The Icy Grave of the H.M.S. *Edinburgh*

Today, the era of treasure fleets sailing the oceans is long gone. During both World Wars, however, nations on both sides transported gold and other treasure overseas to their allies.

The Soviet Union entered World War II in 1941. Britain agreed to send its new ally much-needed shipments of food and military supplies, which the Soviets paid for in gold. The ships left from Scotland or Iceland, traveled across the Arctic Ocean, and docked in the northwest Soviet port of Murmansk. They traveled in convoys protected by destroyers and other warships. The route was so dangerous that sailors nicknamed it "Suicide Run." Ships were in constant risk of attack by the enemy's ships, U-boat submarines, and airplanes. The arctic weather, too, could be fatal. Sheets of ice formed on the ships, sometimes growing so massive that ships were in danger of growing top-heavy and capsizing.

The H.M.S. *Edinburgh* was the flagship of one of these British convoys. On April 29, 1942, the warship left Murmansk to return to Britain carrying 850 passengers and a cargo of five and a half tons of Soviet gold. The next day, a U-boat spied the ship. The *Edinburgh* had made the mistake of traveling ahead of the rest of the convoy. The submarine tracked it for five hours before hitting the ship with two torpedoes. The *Edinburgh* was disabled, but it managed to continue for two more days, until German destroyers mounted another attack. Completely crippled, the ship was evacuated. In order to prevent the *Edinburgh* from falling into German hands, the convoy's admiral ordered one of the accompanying British destroyers to torpedo the mangled ship. Since fifty-seven men died in the incident, the ship was later designated a war grave.

German U-boats terrorized the oceans during World War II. Here, a U-boat captured in the Atlantic flies a white flag as it is brought into a British port.

In the 1970s, Keith Jessop—a British oil-rig diver and former Royal Marine—mounted an unsuccessful search for the *Edinburgh.* Undeterred by his failure, Jessop organized another expedition in 1981, this time as part of a partnership and with the approval of the British and Soviet governments.

This time, Jessop's team located the wreck after only ten days. His next step was the recovery of the gold—820 feet (250 meters) deep in the frigid sea, amid wreckage including potentially live ammunition. The salvage work was meticulously planned. Divers prepared by spending two days in a pressurized chamber, gradually becoming accustomed to the high pressure they would experience underwater. They were then lowered to the wreck. Their diving suits were heated by circulating hot water, and they breathed a mixture of oxygen and helium. In between diving shifts, the crew lived in an underwater, pressurized chamber. After spending several days at the wreck, they would return to the surface and spend a week in a decompression chamber.

The salvage work took five weeks. The divers began by cutting an entrance into the side of the ship with torches. For two weeks, they cleared away debris blocking access to the bomb room where the gold was stored. At last, one of the divers picking up debris realized that he had just grabbed a gold bar. They then began the retrieval of the 465 gold bars on the *Edinburgh*. The divers retrieved 431 before a gale forced them to suspend work.

At the time of the salvage, the gold was worth $91 million. In accordance with Jessop's agreement, the British and Soviet government received 55 percent of the treasure. Jessop's share was worth $3.5 million.

In 1986, one of Jessop's partner companies in the expedition returned to retrieve the remaining thirty-four bars of gold.

The Japanese Submarine *I-52*

In 1944, the Japanese submarine *I-52* set out on its maiden voyage. It was bound to deliver its cargo—raw materials and two tons of gold—to the Germans. At 365 feet (111 meters) long,

A flotilla of Japanese submarines lay idle in the bay of Kure Naval Base, near Hiroshima, in 1945. The *I-52* was built in the Kure shipyard.

the *I-52* was Japan's largest submarine. On June 23, the *I-52* surfaced in the middle of the Atlantic Ocean for a rendezvous with a German submarine. The *I-52* picked up German technicians who would install high-tech radar equipment necessary for a particularly hazardous stretch of the journey ahead.

The *I-52* never completed its voyage, however. The Americans had broken the code for the communications between Japan and Germany, and the U.S. Navy was on the watch. A bomber spotted the *I-52* before it had a chance to dive. The pilot dropped two bombs and a torpedo on the submarine, and the *I-52* sank to the ocean floor.

In the early 1990s, Vietnam veteran and shipwreck researcher Paul Tidwell became fascinated with the lost *I-52*. By April 1995, he had put together an expedition using a Russian ship, the *Yuzhmorgeologiya*, and Russian equipment, but because of contamination in the fuel, they were only able to explore the site for about two weeks. Day after day, they found nothing. Tidwell began to worry that the *I-52* had somehow escaped the bomber attack.

As time was running out, Tidwell and his team decided to search a new site suggested by a computer analysis of the information about the sinking of the *I-52* in the original 1944 logs. On the second to last day of the expedition, a sonar scan located the wreckage of the *I-52*. It lay at a depth of 17,000 feet (5,182 meters)—over three miles.

In 1999, Tidwell returned to the *I-52*, this time with two mini-submersibles, the *Mir I* and the *Mir II*. These vessels would be used for exploration. The team conducted the investigation of the wreck with great care and respect, since the wreck was the war grave of the Japanese crew and German technicians. During trips down to the submarine, the manipulator arms of the *Mir I* and the *Mir II* collected personal artifacts and items of cargo. They also retrieved a box that proved to hold not gold but opium, which had been intended for the production of painkillers.

Tidwell concluded that the gold was located in the hull of the submarine, which was intact. There are no definite plans to continue the salvage. The gold in the *I-52* could be worth $20 million or more, but it would cost millions just to cut into the hull. There has also been discussion of raising the *I-52*, potentially a massive and unprecedented project.

Searching for Buried Treasure

3

There are opportunities for treasure hunters on land as well as underwater. Some hidden treasure has yet to be recovered over the centuries. Ancient treasure has been forgotten. Items that were once considered worthless are now prized for their historical or artistic value. One example is the "warbirds"— warplanes that were downed in conflicts and abandoned.

Although most mining for precious metals and gems is done by large operations, individuals can still conduct their own hunts. High-tech breakthroughs present new opportunities for treasure hunters, yet age-old methods can still lead to success. Just as the forty-niners made their fortune in the California gold rush, treasure hunters still strike it rich searching for gold or gems. Modern-day prospectors can pan for gold or hunt a likely site with a metal detector. Amateurs interested in testing their mining skills can search for gems in places such as Arkansas's Crater of Diamonds State Park. In 1924, the site yielded a diamond larger than forty carats in size. In recent years, meteorites have also become highly prized by museums and collectors.

Travis Christner of Richmond, Michigan, prospects for diamonds in Arkansas's Crater of Diamonds State Park, the world's only "finders keepers" diamond mine. In 2006, he and his wife found a ¼ carat brown diamond.

Legends of Lost Treasure

Near mythic stories still abound about lost sources of treasure, and treasure hunters with the resources and imagination still pursue those legendary troves. One of the earlier legends has its origins in the Bible. King Solomon of Jerusalem possessed legendary wealth—his mines supplied him with tons of gold. His gold was mined in a place called Ophir. There is no record of Ophir's location, however, or even any indication of whether it was a single mine or an entire gold field. People have searched for King Solomon's mines, and some people even claim to

The Money Pit

In Robert Louis Stevenson's *Treasure Island*, as well as in many other tales, an intrepid treasure hunter finds a map with an "X" marking the site of untold wealth. In real life, however, pirates rarely buried their plundered treasures. This does not stop some treasure hunters from looking.

Oak Island, Nova Scotia—along Canada's Atlantic Coast—is an extreme example of buried treasure mania. In 1795, three boys exploring the island came across a giant oak tree with an old pulley dangling from a limb. They started digging in the soft soil underneath. Two feet (.6 meters) below the surface, they found a layer of flagstones. At 10 feet (3 meters), they encountered a platform of oak logs. They continued digging to 30 feet (9 meters), at which point they gave up.

Since then, a steady stream of treasure hunters and investors have tried to solve the mystery of Oak Island. They have unearthed more layers of timbers placed every 10 feet (3 meters), as well as layers of charcoal, coconut fiber once used for packing, and ship's putty.

In the nineteenth century, searchers digging to 93 feet (28 meters) opened a hidden tunnel connected to a cunning network of underground passages linked to the sea. As the tide rose,

Robert Louis Stevenson's classic novel *Treasure Island* has fired the imaginations of readers since its publication in 1883. The son of a lighthouse keeper, Stevenson grew up listening to tales of pirates and their plunder.

the shaft filled with water and flooded the entire excavation. Attempts throughout the years to block these flood tunnels have failed, as have attempts to dig around them.

In the more than two hundred years since excavations began on the site, tens of millions of dollars have been spent and six lives have been lost trying to solve the riddle of Oak Island. Three links of chain, a whistle, a pair of scissors, a scrap of parchment paper, and a stone inscribed with a mysterious message have all been found, but nothing of true value.

have found them, but nobody has found a site rich enough to produce enough gold for a modern-day King Solomon.

Seekers of fortune also continue to be fascinated by the treasure of El Dorado. In some versions of the story, it was a king's rich offering to the gods. In others, it was a valley lined with gold. The story grew every time it was repeated. Treasure hunters seeking El Dorado eventually became convinced that it was located in Lake Guatavita, in Colombia. In the early twentieth century, British treasure hunters drained the lake completely, but the bottom hardened and the lake waters rose once again before they could explore. Colombia has since banned treasure hunters from Lake Guatavita. Despite such failures, people still chase after unlikely stories of lost treasure in the belief that they can be the ones to finally reveal the truth and retrieve the riches.

Another legendary source of gold is the Lost Dutchman mine in the Superstition Mountains of Arizona. Most versions of the story contend that the Peralta family originally opened the mine in the

1840s but abandoned it after an Apache ambush. Some years later, Jacob Walz began working a site in the mountains, and many people suspected that he had found the lost mine. (Consistent with the slang of the time, the "Dutchman" was actually German; the German-language word for "German" is *Deutsch*.) Walz died in 1891 without revealing the truth, and the legend subsequently grew. Some claimed that Walz had given them clues about the location; others followed sketchy maps belonging to the Peralta family. In 1931, one treasure hunter was found shot in the head. He had jotted down cryptic notes in his notebook. So far, nobody has found the elusive mine.

Stories about Nazi gold add a modern twist to the age-old stories of lost treasure. As Adolf Hitler extended Nazi rule across Europe, he raided the riches of the nations he conquered. The Nazis seized hundreds of millions of dollars worth of treasure. Then, as Germany began to fall to the Allied forces, they hid one hundred tons of gold in a potassium mine, where it eventually came into the hands of the advancing Americans. A lesser hoard was buried and also eventually retrieved by the Americans. Individual Nazis seized shares for themselves. In 1945, the Russians occupied Germany's main state bank. There is still a fortune in Nazi assets—including gold—that is unaccounted for. Some people steadfastly believe that there is more waiting to be unearthed.

In some cases, a hunt for legendary treasure has ended in success. Edith May Pretty of East Anglia, England, had heard stories that there was treasure in the mounds on her property. In 1938, she hired an archaeologist to investigate. In the spring of 1939, he excavated the tomb of an Anglo-Saxon king. The burial site yielded two dozen pieces of priceless gold and garnet jewelry, gold coins, and other valuable artifacts. When the discovery was publicized, a court took up the matter to determine whether the treasure belonged to Pretty or to the government. The jury ruled in favor of Pretty, who immediately donated the entire find to the British Museum.

The Nazis pillaged the art and riches of the territories they conquered during World War II. This gold ingot bears a Nazi stamp.

The Pyre of the *Kee Bird*

Just as there are fanatics fascinated with shipwrecks and lost treasure, there are enthusiasts obsessed with "warbirds"—vintage fighter planes. Many of the warbirds still in existence today were downed during World War II or other military operations. Once considered obsolete, and thus useless for anything but scrap metal, these planes are now prized by aircraft and war history

Warbird enthusiasts flock to airshows where vintage warplanes return to the skies. Here, a P-40 Kittyhawk lifts off during the Warbirds over Wanaka International Airshow in New Zealand.

buffs. Warbird enthusiasts mount helicopter searches for downed warbirds, pore over records, and interview present-day residents for leads. In some cases, when they locate a warbird, salvagers bring the aircraft back from the grave. Museums and collectors are willing to pay millions for some planes.

Like deep sea expeditions, searches for this "winged treasure" can be expensive, uncertain, and risky. One of these epic efforts was the doomed expedition to recover the *Kee Bird*.

On February 20, 1947, the *Kee Bird* departed Anchorage, Alaska, for a secret mission in the frozen Arctic. The *Kee Bird* was a Boeing B-29 Superfortress, a newly developed aircraft that at the time was among the most powerful and complex airplanes ever manufactured. It was 90 feet (27 meters) long and had a wingspan of 141 feet (43 meters). At the time, tensions were heightening between the United States and the Soviet Union in anticipation of the Cold War. Speculating that the Soviet Union might use Arctic islands and floes as military bases, the Strategic Air Command launched a project to map and photograph the Arctic. The *Kee Bird*'s crew was instructed to scope out and photograph a certain ice floe.

The airmen reached their target successfully, and they headed back shortly after midnight. It was a cloudy night, and their flight was turbulent. By dawn, the men realized that they were lost—and running low on fuel. The pilot prepared to make an emergency landing on a glacier.

Back in Alaska, the air force had been tracing the *Kee Bird*'s flight and thus was aware when it crashed in northern Greenland. On February 24, in a daring rescue, a small plane called the *Red Raider* landed on ice near the *Kee Bird* and retrieved the eleven crew members, all unhurt. The *Kee Bird*, however, was abandoned.

In the summer of 1993, a group of warbird enthusiasts, led by Gary Larkins and Darryl Greenamyer, took a reconnaissance trip by helicopter to check out the *Kee Bird*. They found that the plane was beautifully preserved.

Larkins was renowned as a salvager of crashed planes. If anyone could free the huge *Kee Bird* from its resting place in a Greenland lake, Larkins would be the one. But how would the group transport a Boeing Superfortress trapped in the Arctic Circle? The only way, Larkins concluded, was to fly it out.

It was a costly and arduous undertaking. The first step was to determine whether their project was feasible. After being exposed to the elements for over forty years, the plane's controls could be too corroded to repair. The group shoveled away tons of frigid mud and used hydraulic jacks to raise the plane out of the shallow water. Greenamyer, an aircraft expert and former test pilot, hooked the electrical system up to a battery. They were able to get the engine started. The group left Greenland feeling confident about their prospects.

Their plan was to spend the summer of 1994 replacing the engines and tuning up the *Kee Bird*. They projected that within three weeks, the *Kee Bird* could be prepared to take flight. But since the Greenland summer lasted only a month, time was tight.

The team flew in tons of new parts for the *Kee Bird*, as well as tools, fuel, camping gear, supplies, a crane for hoisting, and a bulldozer to create a runway. They began their work in frigid temperatures, sometimes having to endure high winds and gusting snow. The repairs proceeded smoothly, but the weather started to deteriorate before the *Kee Bird* was ready to fly. Worse, Rick Kriege, the airplane mechanic who was to act as the *Kee Bird*'s flight engineer, became sick. Greenamyer made the decision to abandon the effort before they were locked in by the weather. Kriege was rushed to the hospital and diagnosed with a rare blood disease. He died about two weeks later.

After three years of restoration in frigid Greenland, the *Kee Bird* burst into flames on an improvised runway on May 26, 1995.

The next year, Greenamyer returned to the *Kee Bird*. The team was able to bring the plane back to life, and they deemed that she was flyable. With Greenamyer at the controls, the *Kee Bird* rushed down the rough runway. Before she was aloft, though, flames erupted in the tail of the plane due to a fuel spill. Greenamyer was nearly trapped by a jammed seatbelt mechanism. Within hours, the *Kee Bird* burned down to a molten shell, with nothing left for salvage.

The prize of a lifetime was lost, but passion for the warbirds of World War II remains high. Enthusiasts scour the far north and the islands of the Pacific for wrecks and sometimes even locate wrecks in Europe and the western United States. There are still plenty of warbirds waiting.

So You Want to Be a Treasure Hunter

4

Treasure fever can tempt armchair treasure hunters into fantasizing about dropping everything just to hop into a boat and begin the search for gold. But don't reach for your goggles and flippers too quickly. A successful treasure hunt can be the adventure of a lifetime, but it begins with research and often ends in a court of law. In between, a treasure hunter faces a huge array of challenges on land as well as on sea. In addition to locating elusive wrecks and battling stormy weather, a treasure hunter must raise the money to mount the expedition and meticulously plan a major operation. Professional treasure hunters have long years of experience.

Know Your History

Which ship should you hunt for? According to some estimates, there are three million wrecks in the ocean, with Spanish treasure alone worth $100 billion. Since it can cost millions to conduct a major expedition, a treasure hunter must begin

The search for information can lead treasure hunters to a wide variety of sources, from online databases to military records and historical archives.

by determining whether salvaging a certain wreck can yield a profit. A ship's manifest—the cargo list—can indicate the value aboard the wreck. Historical descriptions of the wreck will tell whether the ship sank offshore or deep in the ocean, which would be much more difficult to salvage.

Clues from historical records can help narrow down the search area for a specific wreck. A treasure hunter will pore over historical records, maps, official reports, media accounts, descriptions of previous salvage attempts, and whatever other sources are available. If it's an old wreck, this may entail deciphering archaic terminology and handwriting—sometimes in a different language. Treasure hunters also consult with experts and, if the wreck is close to the shore, talk with residents of the area.

Despite most professional treasure hunters' expertise in the field, there has been a long-held animosity between treasure hunters and archaeologists, historians, and academics. These groups believe that shipwrecks are a priceless cultural treasure, not a potential fortune. Traditionally, they have argued that professional treasure hunters destroy archaeological sites and damage artifacts during their salvage work.

Treasure hunters counter that wreck expeditions are so expensive that without the payoff at the end, nobody would put up the money to finance the exploration. They also point out that many shipwrecks are deteriorating over time, and if every one had to wait for a proper archaeological excavation, some would never be explored. Today, treasure hunters and academics share more in common than they did in the past. Most professional treasure-hunting operations include archaeologists on their teams.

"Sport divers" who visit wrecks as a hobby or a sideline fall into another category. Many sport divers follow the creed "Take only pictures and leave only bubbles." They advocate the preservation of shipwrecks, and in some cases, they can contribute valuable information about wrecks. At their worst, however, sport divers are looters who strip sites bare of historical artifacts. In any case, human activities such as shorefront construction projects, dredging, and fishing cause far more destruction to shipwrecks than sport divers.

Know the Law by Sea

In nearly every high-stakes treasure salvage, the treasure hunters have to defend their claim to the treasure in legal battles. The state of Florida, and subsequently the federal government, challenged Mel Fisher's right to the treasure of the *Atocha*. Barry Clifford fought against the state of Massachusetts, which tried to claim a significant percentage of the *Whydah*'s treasure. Thirty-nine insurance companies who had covered the *Central America*'s cargo filed a claim for the treasure salvaged by Tommy Thompson.

The treasure hunters won in these cases, but rulings don't always favor their side. A group called the Sea Search Armada spent $10 million searching for the Spanish treasure ship the

San Jose. They identified a likely wreck off the coast of Colombia, but exploration ceased when the Colombian government claimed the rights to the bulk of any treasure that might be recovered. The case is still being contested. Legal issues can also stymie archaeologists who are interested in the historical value of a find, not the treasure. In the early 1980s, Robert F. Marx began planning an investigation of what he believed was a Roman ship in the Bay of Guanabara, Brazil. The Brazilian government denied permission to excavate, however, and used a dredge ship to cover over the site.

Treasure hunters often discover that navigating salvage law can be one of the most frustrating aspects of their search. Shipwrecks lying in water within a nation's boundaries fall within that country's jurisdiction, and salvage law varies greatly from one nation to another. Within the United States, laws also vary from one state to another. There is even less agreement over rights to wrecks in international waters.

Ownership of the wreck can also be an issue. Before a treasure hunter can get a permit to search for or investigate a wreck, he or she may have to prove that the ship has been abandoned by its original owners. This can be murky legal territory. The United States, for example, claims ownership of lost American warships anywhere in the world. A prospective treasure hunter should thoroughly research the history of a ship before launching a search.

Even after treasure hunters have acquired the necessary permits and located the wreck, they must offer proof of their

NATIONAL GEOGRA

C EXPLORER

PRESENTS

Quest for

the Atoch

REMIERING ON

STATION WT

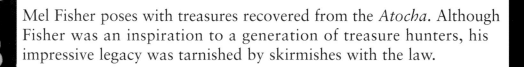

Mel Fisher poses with treasures recovered from the *Atocha*. Although Fisher was an inspiration to a generation of treasure hunters, his impressive legacy was tarnished by skirmishes with the law.

findings—by retrieving an artifact, for example—before being granted salvage rights. They are then named "salvor in possession," which gives them claim to the wreck.

Know the Law by Land

Land-based treasure hunters also need to learn about local, state, and federal laws. Buried treasure with no known owner— whether it's a pile of gold coins or valuable artifacts—is known legally as a "treasure trove" and generally belongs to the finder. In many parks, metal detecting and digging may require a permit, or it might be banned altogether. Treasure hunting is also forbidden in some places due to preservation laws, such as the American Antiquities Act of 1906 and the National Historic Preservation Act of 1966. Needless to say, laws vary greatly in every country, so anyone planning a search for South American gold or King Solomon's mines should research the law before packing for the trip.

Mounting an Expedition

Before would-be treasure hunters can take to the sea, they must find investors for the project. An expedition typically requires millions of dollars. Therefore, a treasure hunter must also be an accomplished salesman and fund-raiser, someone who can infect others with treasure fever. Since treasure hunts often encounter unexpected snags or drag on longer than

The Amber Room

Although "treasure" is usually thought of as precious metal, art and currency also qualify as treasure. A hunt for lost art can be even more uncertain than a search for gold and silver, though, because art is more easily destroyed.

During World War II, the Nazis seized a fortune in artwork. As the German army advanced on the Soviet Union, the curators of Leningrad's art museums and palaces sent their collections to safety in Siberia. One of Russia's greatest treasures, though, was too fragile to transport. This was the magnificent Amber Room, constructed in 1701. Its walls were paneled in amber that had been heated, flattened, dyed, and pieced together.

The Amber Room was never seen again after the war ended, despite many efforts to trace it. Two of the treasure hunters who recently investigated the fate of the Amber Room were journalists Catherine Scott-Clark and Adrian Levy. They followed the trail of the

German chancellor Gerhard Schröder and Russian president Vladimir Putin attend the 2003 opening of the reconstructed Amber Room in the Catherine Palace of St. Petersburg.

Amber Room to Germany's Königsburg Castle, to which German soldiers supposedly transported dismantled pieces of the room. In 1945, at the end of the war, the Soviet army stormed the city of Königsburg. Scott-Clark and Levy believe that the Amber Room was destroyed in a fire carelessly set as Soviet soldiers looted the city.

Nevertheless, their conclusion is only one of many theories on the fate of this masterpiece. Undoubtedly, treasure hunters will continue to chase after possible leads to the Amber Room for many years to come. In the meantime, those who are interested can view the reconstruction of the original Amber Room built by the Russian government in 2003.

anticipated, raising money can be an ongoing concern throughout the expedition.

A treasure hunter must also manage a team of divers and other experts involved in the exploration and recovery. In the early days of scuba diving, when very few people had taken up the sport, Mel Fisher recruited his fellow diving buddies to join him on the *Atocha* hunt. Today, tightly organized salvage companies hire professional divers for their treasure hunts.

Since every day spent searching adds to the expense of the expedition, a treasure hunter must plan and prepare for every stage of the expedition well in advance. He or she must also have contingency plans in case of mishaps or complications. During the salvage of the *Edinburgh*, Keith Jessop juggled the logistics of having a rotating team of divers who spent time in multiple compression and decompression chambers. Tommy

Thompson designed an ROV specifically for the salvage of the *Central America* in advance of the recovery effort.

The field of treasure hunting is highly competitive. During the hunt for the *Atocha*, Mel Fisher raced to locate the ship against Burt Webber, another accomplished treasure hunter. Treasure hunters keep their plans and progress secret, sometimes to an obsessive degree. Once they have located a wreck, they are unwilling to divulge any specifics about the location in order to keep looters away.

Studying to Be a Treasure Hunter

Many of the most famous treasure hunters did not prepare for their career in school. Mel Fisher started out as a chicken farmer. Kip Wagner was a home builder. Tommy Thompson, however, had a degree in engineering. If, as is the current trend, treasure-hunting operations continue to take a more systematic archaeological approach to salvage work, they may look for employees with backgrounds in science, engineering, archaeology, history, or other related fields.

If you're an aspiring treasure hunter, pay attention in school and give your sense of curiosity a free rein. Treasure hunters must be well grounded in most school subjects, especially geography, history, science, and math. A treasure hunter should be articulate, since he or she will have to persuade investors to join the project. Divers must be physically fit. If

Landbound treasure hunters can employ a metal detector to find artifacts such as coins and jewelry, and also to gain a new perspective on the history of their area in the process.

you live near the ocean, you can follow Kip Wagner's example and comb the beach for artifacts. Even if you live hours away from the ocean, you can invest in a metal detector, grab a trowel, and do some urban exploration of parks and the sites of old buildings. (Just make sure that you know the law and take sensible safety precautions.)

Treasure hunters don't start out by leading high-stakes expeditions. The first step is to learn how to swim and scuba dive. Divers who are interested in specializing in wreck diving can take a certification course that teaches how to avoid some of the dangers particular to shipwrecks. Novice treasure hunters generally start out by working on the team of an experienced treasure hunter.

You don't necessarily have to be a diver in order to be part of a treasure hunting expedition. If you ever happen to be looking for an investment opportunity and an adventure at the same time, check out a reputable treasure-hunting operation. If you want to participate from a safe distance, you could specialize in historical research of shipwrecks. Treasure hunters bring up the gold, silver, and artifacts, but they need experts such as preservationists to clean and restore each item.

Glossary

amber A translucent, yellowish brown fossilized resin that is used in making jewelry.

archaeology The study of prehistoric and historic human culture through the recovery and analysis of material remains such as artifacts, buildings, and inscriptions.

artifact An object made by human craft, especially one of archaeological interest.

ballast Heavy material placed in a ship to provide stability.

concretion In geology, a mass of mineral matter, often formed around a central nucleus.

convoy A group of vehicles traveling together, often for safety.

fleet A group of ships or other vehicles under the same ownership or command.

galleon A large square-rigged sailing ship with three masts that was used from the fifteenth to the eighteenth century, especially by Spain.

hull The frame or body of a ship.

hypothermia Abnormally low body temperature.

magnetometer An instrument that detects the presence of ferrous metallic objects.

maritime Of or relating to shipping or navigation on the sea.

remotely operated vehicle (ROV) An unmanned underwater vessel that is controlled from a ship.

salvor One who salvages a ship or its cargo.

submersible A vessel capable of operating underwater.

trove Treasure of unknown ownership found hidden, usually in the earth.

For More Information

British Museum
Great Russell Street
London WC1B 3DG
England
+44 (0)20 7323 8000/8299
E-mail: information@britishmuseum.org
Web site: http://www.britishmuseum.org
The British Museum holds one of the world's greatest collections
of art and artifacts.

Institute of Nautical Archaeology
P.O. Drawer HG
College Station, TX 77841-5137
(979) 845-6694
E-mail: ina@tamu.edu
Web site: http://ina.tamu.edu
This underwater archaeological research organization was
founded by the underwater archaeologist George Bass.

The Maritime Museum of the Atlantic
1675 Lower Water Street
Halifax, NS B3J 1S3
Canada
(902) 424-7490
Web site: http://museum.gov.ns.ca/mma/index.html
The museum's collection includes artifacts, images, charts, and
plans relating to the marine history of Nova Scotia. The
Royal Canadian Navy, the Canadian merchant marine,
Nova Scotia small craft, and local shipwrecks are particular
strengths of the collection, much of which represents the
period of 1850 to the present.

National Underwater and Marine Agency (NUMA)
P.O. Box 5059
Scottsdale, AZ 85258
Web site: http://www.numa.net
Founded by the best-selling author Clive Cussler, NUMA is a
nonprofit, volunteer foundation dedicated to preserving
maritime heritage through the discovery, archaeological
survey, and conservation of shipwreck artifacts.

Naval Historical Center
Washington Navy Yard
805 Kidder Breese Street SE
Washington Navy Yard, DC 20374-5060

(202) 433-7880

Web site: http://www.history.navy.mil

As the official history program of the United States Navy, the Naval Historical Center manages the Navy Department Library, twelve navy museums, art collections, archives, and an underwater archaeology program.

Northern Maritime Research

P.O. Box 48047

Bedford, NS B4A 3Z2

Canada

(902) 445-5497

E-mail: info@NorthernMaritimeResearch.com

Web site: http://www.northernmaritimeresearch.com

Over the last twenty-six years, Northern Maritime Research has accumulated a database of more than 100,000 North American shipwrecks covering 400 years.

UNESCO—the United Nations Educational, Scientific and Cultural Organization

United States Liaison Office

2 United Nations Plaza, Room 900

New York, NY 10017

(212) 963-5995

E-mail: newyork@unesco.org

Web site: http://www.unesco.org

UNESCO promotes international cooperation among its 193 member states and six associate members in the fields of education, science, culture, and communication.

Web Sites

Due to the changing nature of Internet links, Rosen Publishing has developed an online list of Web sites related to the subject of this book. This site is updated regularly. Please use this link to access the list:

http://www.rosenlinks.com/exc/trhu

For Further Reading

Ballard, Robert B. *Ghost Liners: Exploring the World's Greatest Lost Ships.* Boston, MA: Little, Brown, 1998.

Claybourne, Anna, et al. *The Usborne Book of Treasure Hunting.* Tulsa, OK: E.D.C. Publishing, 1999.

Holub, Joan. *How to Find Treasure in All Fifty States and Canada Too!* New York, NY: Aladdin Paperbacks, 2000.

Konstam, Angus. *The History of Shipwrecks.* Guilford, CT: Lyons Press, 2002.

Matsen, Bradford. *The Incredible Search for the Treasure Ship Atocha.* Berkeley Heights, NJ: Enslow Publishers, 2003.

Pickford, Nigel. *The Atlas of Shipwrecks and Treasure: The History, Location, and Treasures of Ships Lost at Sea.* New York, NY: Dorling Kindersley, 1994.

Potter, John S., Jr. *The Treasure Diver's Guide.* New York, NY: Doubleday, 1960.

Stevenson, Robert Louis. *Treasure Island.* London, England: Bloomsbury Publishing, 2006.

Thompson, Tommy. *America's Lost Treasure.* New York, NY: Atlantic Monthly Press, 1998.

Bibliography

Chaplan, Michael. *The Urban Treasure Hunter: A Practical Handbook for Beginners*. Garden City Park, NY: Square One Publishers, 2005.

Clifford, Barry, with Peter Turchi. *The Pirate Prince: Discovering the Priceless Treasures of the Sunken Ship Whydah*. New York, NY: Simon and Schuster, 1993.

Gilkes, Martha Watkins. *Shipwrecks of the Caribbean: A Diver's Guide*. New York, NY: Interlink Books, 2003.

Hoffman, Carl. *Hunting Warbirds: The Obsessive Quest for the Lost Aircraft of World War II*. New York, NY: Ballantine Books, 2001.

Johnson, Stephen. *The Complete Idiot's Guide to Sunken Ships and Treasures*. Indianapolis, IN: Alpha Books, 2000.

Kurson, Robert. *Shadow Divers: The True Adventure of Two Americans Who Risked Everything to Solve One of the Last Mysteries of World War II*. New York, NY: Random House, 2004.

Marx, Robert F., with Jenifer Marx. *Treasure Lost at Sea: Diving to the World's Great Shipwrecks.* Buffalo, NY: Firefly Books, 2004.

Ohrelius, Bengt. *Vasa: The King's Ship.* Philadelphia, PA: Chilton Books, 1963.

Pickford, Nigel. *Lost Treasure Ships of the Twentieth Century.* Washington, DC: National Geographic, 1999.

Scott-Clark, Catherine, and Adrian Levy. *The Amber Room: The Fate of the World's Greatest Lost Treasure.* New York, NY: Walker and Company, 2004.

Time-Life eds. *Lost Treasure.* Alexandria, VA: Time-Life Books, 1991.

Trupp, Philip Z. *Tracking Treasure: Romance and Fortune Beneath the Sea and How to Find It!* Washington, DC: Acropolis Books Ltd., 1986.

Index

About the Author

Corona Brezina's single attempt at treasure hunting ended with the discovery of several rusty nails located by a metal detector. She is a writer who has written over a dozen titles for Rosen Publishing. Several of her previous books have explored interesting career possibilities for young adults, including *Careers in Forensics: Medical Examiner*. She lives in Chicago.

Photo Credits

Cover © Time-Life Pictures/Getty Images; pp. 5, 12, 26, 32, 36 © Getty Images; p. 6 © National Geographic/Getty Images; p. 9 © Steve Lindridge/Eye Ubiquitous/Corbis; p. 11, 17, 46 © AP Photos; p. 14 *Which Shall Be Captain?*, from "The Buccaneers," published in *Harper's Monthly Magazine*, 1911 (oil on canvas) by Howard Pyle (1853–1911) © Delaware Art Museum, Wilmington, USA/Gift of Dr. James Stillman/The Bridgeman Art Library; p. 21 © Macduff Everton/Corbis; p. 23 © The Granger Collection; p. 28 © Bettmann/Corbis; p. 31 © *Christian Science Monitor*/Getty Images; p. 35 © Corbis/Sygma; p. 39 © Tim Wright/Corbis; p. 42 © Roger Viollet/Getty Images; p. 48 © AFP/Getty Images; p. 51 Shutterstock.

Designer: Les Kanturek; **Editor:** Peter Herman
Photo Researcher: Marty Levick